The Silence
AND THE
SOUND

A Cantata for Christmas

BY HEATHER SORENSON
ORCHESTRATION BY KEITH CHRISTOPHER

Performance Time: ca. 45 minutes

① This symbol indicates a track number on the StudioTrax CD (accompaniment only) or SplitTrax CD

ISBN 978-1-4950-1502-1

EXCLUSIVELY DISTRIBUTED BY

HAL•LEONARD®
CORPORATION

7777 W. BLUEMOUND RD. P.O. BOX 13819 MILWAUKEE, WI 53213

In Australia Contact:
Hal Leonard Australia Pty. Ltd.
4 Lentara Court
Cheltenham, Victoria, 3192 Australia
Email: ausadmin@halleonard.com.au

Visit Hal Leonard Online at
www.halleonard.com

Visit Shawnee Press Online at
www.shawneepress.com

FOREWORD

How do you write a cantata about the greatest event in history? How do you capture th
awesomeness of Redemption in 45 minutes of human vocabulary? How do you make
and new something that has been told a million times before? I carried the weight of th
questions while writing *The Silence and the Sound.*

I remember sitting in a hotel room in July, looking through Christmas music (we're all
church musicians here – that comment makes perfect sense to us all!), and I read throug
ancient carol "Let All Mortal Flesh Keep Silence." I think that was probably the first ti
I had *really* read and absorbed the text. The impact of the opening lyrics took my breat
away, and the magnitude of Christmas became almost tangible to me. That moment be
the springboard for this cantata, and that carol became the anchor.

And so now, I'm "passing the torch" to your choir: may you experience and communic:
the awe of silence, the humility of Redemption, and the shout of joy during this Christn
season.

Merry Christmas!

– Heather Sorenson

PERFORMANCE NOTES

This (approximately) 45-minute work includes the following elements:

- SATB choir
- Children's chorus (or optional child solo)
- Several soloists
- Two adult narrators
- Two child readers (optional)

Let All Mortal Flesh Keep Silence
This piece has small narrations throughout the song. The same narrator should read
all of the narration in this piece. Please refer to the score for narrator entrances.

Come To Us
This piece begins with a child soloist (recommended), but you may wish to use an
adult female instead.

Luke 2
This is the traditional reading of the Christmas story, underscored by piano (or
orchestra) and the adult choir. Having two children reading the story would be a
special touch, but two adults would work just as well. You could even use the two
adult narrators, or possibly even just one reader.

Sleeping Adonai

Start this piece immediately at the end of Luke 2. This song is a lullaby, so the soloist should not "over-sing" it. Allow the piece to breathe, and sing it gently as if you were holding a sleeping infant.

Angels Sing

The narration leading up to this piece serves as a bridge, transitioning from the previous lullaby to angels singing joyfully. The narrator should build excitement in his/her voice to set up "Angels Sing." The children's chorus is the anchor for this piece. If you do not have a children's chorus, a child soloist will work fine. The song was written in simplicity to teach children the story of Christmas, as well as introduce them to traditional Christmas carols. If you wish, the children could all be dressed in Biblical costumes: shepherds, wise men, Mary and Joseph, animals, and the star. Who doesn't love kids in costumes at Christmas?!

Unto Us

The narration leading into this song has an underscore that helps create an intimate setting. The narrators should read warmly and conversationally. This alto/tenor duet creates a powerful moment of personal reflection in the cantata. Because the piece is somewhat more contemporary stylistically, the soloists should feel free to ad-lib if they would like, although that is not necessary for the success of the piece.

Shout! Sing Hallelujah!

In the narration leading up to this song, it is critical that the narrators build excitement in their voices all the way to the end. An underscore begins halfway through the narration, and helps to build momentum. When Narrator 1 enters with "Our Christmas silence has ended," he/she should enter with the same excitement level that Narrator 2 has ended, so that there is no dip in energy. Continue building excitement from there. This is the "Sound" moment in *The Silence and the Sound*, so don't let it fall flat!

Worship Christ the King

Start this piece immediately after "Shout! Sing Hallelujah!" If you wish, you may end the cantata with this piece. The last portion of the medley is a reprise of "Let All Mortal Flesh Keep Silence," creating a full-circle moment with a natural finale.

A Tribute of Carols

This piece is an optional choir and congregational sing-a-long (program inserts for congregation are on pages 111-112). I find that many congregants are in such a state of worship at the end of cantatas that they want to join their own praise with the choir. This carol medley gives them that perfect opportunity. If you prefer to end the cantata with "Worship Christ the King," you may wish to open your cantata service with "A Tribute of Carols" instead, for a time of corporate worship with your congregation.

4

(MUSIC FOR "LET ALL MORTAL FLESH KEEP SILENCE" BEGINS)

NARRATOR 1:

The time had come. The time when eternity would be altered forever.
This was the moment when condemnation would meet redemption.
When the free reign of darkness would meet the Light of the World.

The time was now. And as the curtains rolled back from a divinely-set
stage, all of creation rose and stood in silence.

(Measure 18)

Let all the world rise and stand in silence.

(Measure 32)

Then the armies of heaven fell into place, lining the pathway for their Prince.

(Measure 48)

As the Prince of Heaven stepped down from His throne, the angelic beings
shielded their eyes, so as not to even gaze upon His holiness.

LET ALL MORTAL FLESH KEEP SILENCE

for S.A.T.B. voices, accompanied

Words: Liturgy of St. James, 5th c.;
tr. Gerard Moultrie, 1864

Tune: **PICARDY**
French carol, 17th c.
Arranged by
HEATHER SORENSON (ASCAP)

THE SILENCE AND THE SOUND - SATB

Let all mor-tal flesh keep

TENOR

BASS

si - lence, and with fear and trem - bling stand.

Narr: Let all the world rise and stand in silence.

Si - lence. Pon-der noth-ing earth - ly mind - ed,

for with bless-ing in _____ His _____ hand. Si - lence.

Christ our God to earth de - scend - eth, our full hom-age to _____ de -

mand. Si - lence. Si - lence, let the world keep si - lence. _____

8

Narr: Then the armies of heaven fell into place, lining the pathway for their Prince.

from the realms of end - less__ day, that the pow'rs of hell may

van - ish as the dark - ness clears__ a - way.

48 Ethereal

Narr: As the Prince of Heaven stepped down from His throne, the angelic beings shielded their eyes, so as not to even gaze upon His holiness.

THE SILENCE AND THE SOUND - SATB

in the bod-y and___ the___ blood, the blood. He will give to all the

faith - ful His own self for heav - 'nly___ food.

Slower (♩ = ca. 60)

Al - le - lu - ia, al - le - lu - ia, al - le - lu - ia, Lord___ Most___

Slower (♩ = ca. 60)

NARRATOR 1:

The silence of Christmas began long before the birth of Christ.
For 400 years, God was silent. From the final words of the prophet
Malachi until the proclamation of John the Baptist, from the time
between the Old Testament and the New Testament - there were no
prophecies, no revelations, no direct communications with His children.

What kind of God would leave His people in silence for 400 years?

NARRATOR 2:

A God who keeps His promises. A God whose attention to detail
would not allow the plan of redemption to unfold prematurely.

You see, God is often silent while He is working. During those
400 silent years, God was resetting the world stage. Key prophecies
were being fulfilled. The nations of the world were repositioning
themselves to be in direct alignment with Scripture. For the first
time in history, the Hebrew prophecies were being translated into
another language: the universal Greek language, allowing for
ALL nations to recognize the Messiah - at just the right time.

There was a plan. Galatians 4:4 says, "In the *fullness of time*,
God sent forth His Son to be born of a woman."

NARRATOR 1:

But while the curtain was closed, and while God was silent, His
oppressed children were crying to Him for deliverance.

(SEGUE TO "COME TO US")

COME TO US

for S.A.T.B. voices, accompanied

Words and Music by
HEATHER SORENSON (ASCAP)

THE SILENCE AND THE SOUND - SATB

We have been wait - ing, and need You to come and

save us. _____

(end solo)

8va - - - - -

pp (echo)

Ped. _____

23

S. *mp* unis.

A.

Come to us, Je - sus, and take all our fears a -

T. *mp* unis.

B.

23

mp

save us.   Ah   Hold up the

wea-ry. Lift up the weak.   Help us and give us the

peace that we seek.   You have been prom-ised. We   kneel and we

24

*O come to us, Je - sus, we

ask Thee to stay close by us for - ev - er, and

love us, we pray. Bless all the dear chil - dren in

* Tune: MUELLER, James R. Murray, 1841-1905, alt.; Words: John Thomas McFarland, 1851-1913, alt.

THE SILENCE AND THE SOUND - SATB

NARRATOR 2:

God heard the cries of His people, just as He hears our cries today, and He sent a Deliverer, His only Son: a Savior, who is Christ the Lord.

(MUSIC FOR "LUKE 2" BEGINS)

This reading can be delivered by two children, or by the same adult narrators.

CHILD 1:

And it came to pass in those days, that there went out a decree from Caesar Augustus that all the world should be taxed. And all went to be taxed, every one into his own city.

CHILD 2:

And Joseph also went up from Galilee, out of the city of Nazareth, into Judaea, unto the city of David, which is called Bethlehem; (because he was of the house and lineage of David:) to be taxed with Mary his espoused wife, being great with child.

CHILD 1:

And so it was, that, while they were there, the days were accomplished that she should be delivered. And she brought forth her firstborn son, and wrapped him in swaddling clothes, and laid him in a manger; because there was no room for them in the inn.

CHILD 2:

And there were in the same country shepherds abiding in the field, keeping watch over their flock by night. And lo, the angel of the Lord came upon them, and the glory of the Lord shone round about them; and they were sore afraid. And the angel said unto them, "Fear not: for, behold, I bring you good tidings of great joy, which shall be to all people. For unto you is born this day in the city of David a Savior, which is Christ the Lord. And this shall be a sign unto you; Ye shall find the babe wrapped in swaddling clothes, lying in a manger."

CHILD 1:

And suddenly there was with the angel a multitude of the heavenly host praising God, and saying, "Glory to God in the highest, and on earth peace, good will toward men." And it came to pass, as the angels were gone away from them into heaven, the shepherds said one to another, "Let us now go even unto Bethlehem, and see this thing which is come to pass, which the Lord hath made known unto us." And they came with haste, and found Mary, and Joseph, and the babe lying in a manger.

LUKE 2

with "Silent Night"

for Piano and S.A.T.B. underscore

Tune: **STILLE NACHT**
by FRANZ GRUBER (1787-1863)
Arranged by
HEATHER SORENSON (ASCAP)

Narr: **And it came to pass in those days...**

THE SILENCE AND THE SOUND - SATB

Narr: A Savior, which is Christ the Lord.

SLEEPING ADONAI

for Solo and S.A.T.B. voices, accompanied

Words and Music by
HEATHER SORENSON (ASCAP)

THE SILENCE AND THE SOUND - SATB

Cleanse the lep - er, cleanse my sin, sleep - ing A - do - nai.

Rule the world with truth and grace, Sav - ior of this fal - len race.

In our hearts You'll find a place, sleep - ing A - do - nai,

sleep - ing A - do - nai. Hal - le -

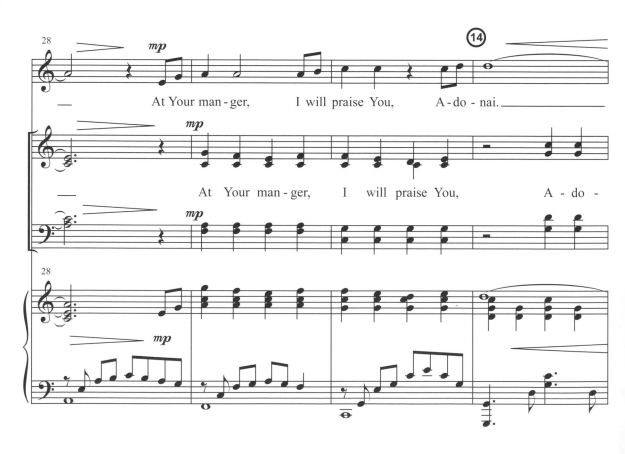

36

Hail the heav'n-born Prince of Peace, hail the Son of Right-eous-ness.

Hail the heav'n-born Prince of Peace, hail the Son of Right-eous-ness.

All the earth will one day bless sleep-ing A-do-nai,

unis.

Sleep-ing A-do-nai,

unis.

38

man - ger,   I will praise You,   A - do - nai.

At   Your   man - ger,   I   will   praise   You,   A - do -

nai.

mf

NARRATOR 1:

Through this sleeping Adonai, the silence of Christmas was beautifully broken. A new Song had been born! The Word became flesh, and came to live among the very people He had created. A symphony of sound began that night that still echoes throughout the world today: from the cries of a tiny infant King to the multitudes of heaven's citizens shouting His praises from the night sky! The time for silence was past, and the time for rejoicing had come!

ANGELS SING

for S.A.T.B. voices and children's choir (or solo), accompanied

Incorporating
"Angels We Have Heard on High"
and "Hark! the Herald Angels Sing"
Arranged by
HEATHER SORENSON (ASCAP)

Original Words and Music by
HEATHER SORENSON (ASCAP)

*Tune: GLORIA, Traditional French carol; Words: Traditional French carol, tr. James Chadwick

THE SILENCE AND THE SOUND - SATB

ri - a!

CHILDREN'S CHOIR (OR SOLO)

17 **Light, joyful**

mf

Shep - herds watched their flocks by night,

Light, joyful

wise men saw a star so bright, proph-ets with their pen did write of

things they'd not yet seen. Af - ter walk - ing days and miles,

S.A. *mp* unis.

Oo _____

Ma - ry had a lit - tle child, Jo - seph and the cat - tle smiled while

all of heav-en beamed. Heav-'nly prais-es ring, "Glo-ry to the King," an-gels

Heav-'nly prais-es ring, "Glo-ry to the King," an-gels

sing.＿＿＿＿＿＿ Glo -

sing.＿＿＿＿＿＿ Glo -

T.B.

*Tune: MENDELSSOHN, Felix Mendelssohn, 1809-1847; Words: Charles Wesley, 1707-1788

(PIANO UNDERSCORE BEGINS)

NARRATOR 1:

Perhaps the most beautiful Christmas phrase ever penned came from the prophet Isaiah, who would never see the Messiah of whom he wrote: "For unto *us*, a Child is born; unto *us* a Son is given."

NARRATOR 2:

Unto *us*. The Messiah wasn't sent to deliver those who were perfect. He didn't come to save the righteous. For there is none who are righteous, not one of us.

NARRATOR 1:

It was our brokenness that touched heaven's heart; it was our neediness that moved the hand of God. Unto *us*.

NARRATOR 2:

Unto people crippled by life. Unto those who have lost hope. Unto the ones who see themselves as damaged.

NARRATOR 1:

Unto those who work hard, yet still struggle to make ends meet. Unto the people who fail the same test again and again. Unto those who hurt.

NARRATOR 2:

Unto those who are paralyzed by their past.

(BEGIN INTRODUCTION TO "UNTO US")

Whether we realize it or not, none of us are without the need of a Savior.

NARRATOR 1:

We are the broken ones. And so, unto *us*, a Child is born.

NARRATOR 2:

Unto *us*, a Son is given.

UNTO US
(Piano underscore)

Music by
HEATHER SORENSON (ASCAP)

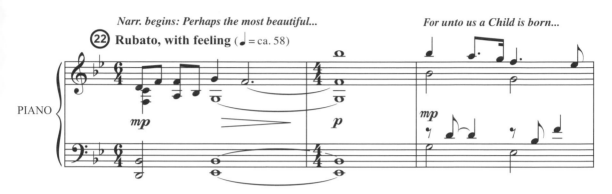

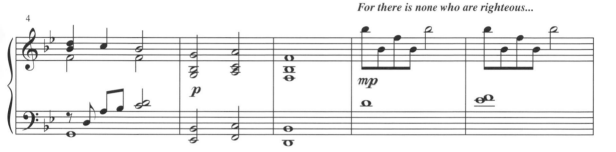

segue into "Unto Us"

UNTO US

for Alto and Tenor solo, with S.A.T.B. voices, accompanied

(MUSIC BEGINS)

Narration: **Whether we realize it or not, none of us are without the need of a Savior. We are the broken ones. And so, unto us a Child is born. Unto us, a Son is given.**

Words and Music by
HEATHER SORENSON (ASCAP)

Un-to us__ a Child is born, un-to us__ He's

58

60

Child is born, right-eous-ness_ has come.__ Ru-ined peo - ple

Child is born, right-eous-ness_ has come.__ Ru-ined peo - ple

to a-tone, our sin be-came_His_ own.__ He did-n't come to save_ the per-

to a-tone, sin be-came_ His_ own.__

come.

If per-fec-tion is__ what God re-quires,__ then count us all__ as lost,__

come. Ah_____

for we have all__ been bro-ken, and there's no one with-out__

Oo_____

NARRATOR 1:

And so this Child, this Messiah, this Savior delivers us today the same way He has delivered His people since Bethlehem: He gives us His own righteousness.

NARRATOR 2:

How can we respond to such an amazing, undeserved gift? We cannot be silent! For if we remain silent, even the rocks will cry out praise in our place. And so we join the great Psalmist in exclaiming:

Bless the Lord, O my soul;
And all that is within me, bless His holy name!
Bless the Lord, O my soul,
And forget not all His benefits:
Who forgives all your iniquities,
Who heals all your diseases,

(MUSIC FOR "SHOUT! SING HALLELUJAH!" UNDERSCORE BEGINS)

Who redeems your life from destruction,
Who crowns you with loving kindness and tender mercies,
Who satisfies your mouth with good things,
*So that your youth is renewed like the eagle's.**

NARRATOR 1:

Our Christmas silence has ended!

So, shout joyfully to the Lord, all the earth;
Break forth in song, rejoice, and sing praises.
Let the sea roar, and all its fullness,
The world and those who dwell in it;
Let the rivers clap their hands;
Let the hills be joyful together before the Lord,
*Shout joyfully to the Lord, all the earth!***

*PSALM 103:1-5, NKJV
**Excerpts from PSALM 98, NKJV

THE SILENCE AND THE SOUND - SATB

SHOUT! SING HALLELUJAH!
(Piano underscore)

Music by
HEATHER SORENSON (ASCAP)

(Narr. cont) Who redeems your life from destruction...

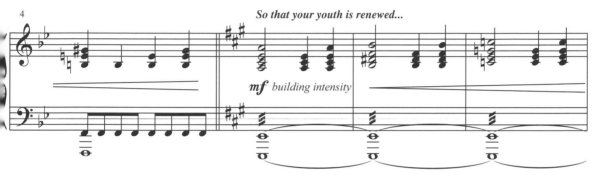

So that your youth is renewed...

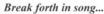

Break forth in song...

Shout joyfully to the Lord, all the earth!

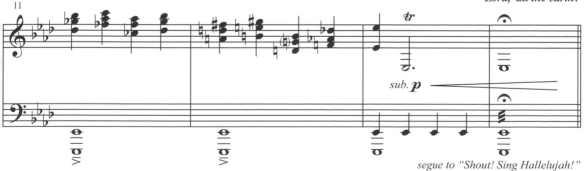

segue to "Shout! Sing Hallelujah!"

THE SILENCE AND THE SOUND - SATB

SHOUT! SING HALLELUJAH!

for S.A.T.B. voices, accompanied

Words and Music by
HEATHER SORENSON (ASCAP)

Shout to God!__ Sing out a hal-le-lu-jah!__ Shout to God!__ Let all the

21
sub. mf
"Praise His name, who life ev - er - last - ing brings!"
sub. mf
21
sub. mf
24
f unis.
30
He's the new - born King!
f unis.
24
f
27
Let the o - ceans clap their hands; moun - tains leap for
27

30
joy; trees bow down and stars a - dore this
30
33
sub. mf
ti - ny, ba - by Boy!
sub. mf
33
sub. mf
36
f unis.
Shout to God! Sing out a hal - le - lu - jah! Shout to God! Let all the
f unis.
36
f

78

a! _____ add vibrato

32 71 accel.

accel.

hal - le - lu - ee - jah!

accel.

De - o. _____

accel.

Peace. _____

71

accel.

73 **Rhythmic** (♩ = ca. 138)

S. *f* unis.

A.

Shout to God! __ Sing out a hal - le - lu - jah! __ Shout to God! __ Let all the

f unis.

T.

B.

73 **Rhythmic** (♩ = ca. 138)

f

82

joy, _____ trees bow down_ and stars a - dore this ti - ny, ba - by Boy! _____

Shout to God!_ Sing out a hal - le - lu - jah!_ Shout to God!_ Let all the

84

world ex - claim: "Praise His name__ who life ev - er - last - ing__

brings!"_____ "Praise His name__ who

life ev - er - last - ing__ brings!" He's the new - born__

THE SILENCE AND THE SOUND - SATB

WORSHIP CHRIST THE KING

for S.A.T.B. voices, accompanied

Arranged by
HEATHER SORENSON (ASCAP)

Incorporating
"O Worship the King,"
"What Child Is This?" *and*
"Let All Mortal Flesh Keep Silence"

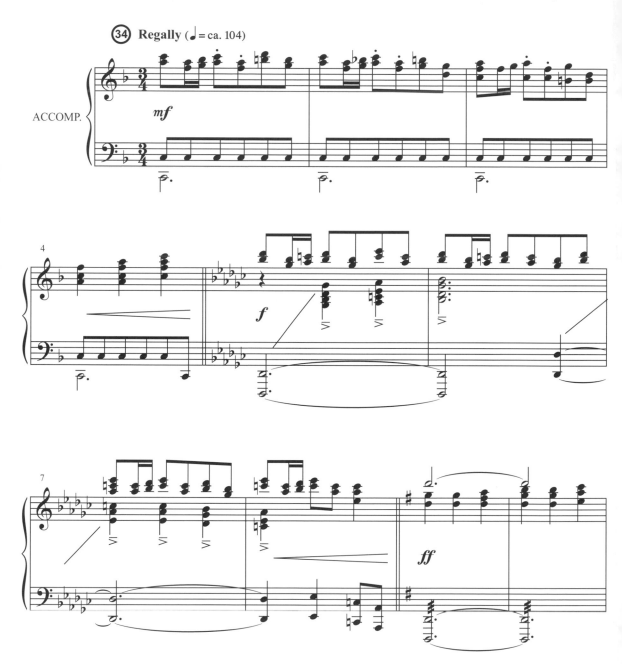

THE SILENCE AND THE SOUND - SATB

*Tune: LYONS, attr. Johann Michael Haydn, 1737-1806; Words: Robert Grant, 1779-1838

THE SILENCE AND THE SOUND - SATB

trust, nor find ___ Thee to fail. Thy

mer - cies, how ten - der, ___

how firm to the

___ our Mak - er, De - fend - er, ___

end,

Re -

94

*Tune: GREENSLEEVES, English melody, 16th c.; Words: William C. Dix, 1837-1898

THE SILENCE AND THE SOUND - SATB

haste to bring Him laud, the Babe, the

to bring Him laud.

Son, Je - sus, the Ho - ly

Je - sus, the Babe, the

One,

*Tune: PICARDY, French melody, 17th c.; Words: Liturgy of St. James, 5th c.

Lord of lords, in hu - man___ ves - ture,

in the bod - y and___ the___ blood, the blood.

He will give to all the faith - ful His own self for heav - 'nly___

A TRIBUTE OF CAROLS

for S.A.T.B. voices with opt. Sop. Descant and Congregation, accompanied

Arranged by
HEATHER SORENSON (ASCAP)

Incorporating
"O Come, All Ye Faithful,"
"Joy to the World!" *and*
"Angels We Have Heard on High"

CHOIR *and* CONGREGATION

O come, all ye faith - ful, joy - ful and tri -

*Tune: ADESTE FIDELES, John F. Wade's *Cantus Diversi*, 1751; Words: Attr. John F. Wade, 1711-1786;
tr. Frederick Oakeley, 1802-1880

THE SILENCE AND THE SOUND - SATB

104

*Joy to the world! the Lord is come; let earth re-ceive her King! Let ev-'ry heart prepare Him room, and

*Tune: ANTIOCH, George Frideric Handel, 1685-1759; Words: Isaac Watts, 1674-1748

THE SILENCE AND THE SOUND - SATB

*Tune: GLORIA, Traditional French carol, 18th c.; Words: Traditional French carol, tr. James Chadwick

THE SILENCE AND THE SOUND - SATB

THE SILENCE AND THE SOUND - SATB

PROGRAM INSERTS FOR CONGREGATIONAL SINGING

"O Come, All Ye Faithful"
ADESTE FIDELES
Words: Attr. John F. Wade (1711-1786), tr. Frederick Oakeley (1802-1880)
Music: John F. Wade's *Cantus Diversi*, 1751

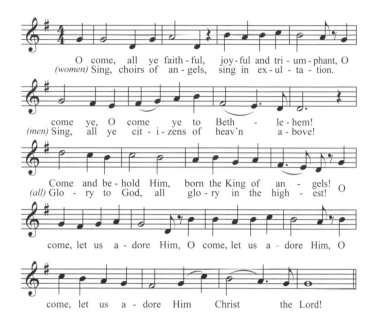

"Joy to the World"
ANTIOCH
Words: Isaac Watts (1674-1748)
Music: George Frideric Handel (1685-1759)

THE SILENCE AND THE SOUND - SATB

"Angels We Have Heard on High"
GLORIA
Words and Music: Traditional French carol, 18th c.
tr. James Chadwick

Glo - - - ri - a! In ex - cel - sis De - o! Glo - ri - a! In ex - cel - sis De - o! Glo - - - ri - a! In ex - cel - sis De - o!